LEVEL
2

Gymnastics

Sarah Wassner Flynn

NATIONAL
GEOGRAPHIC

Washington, D.C.

For Eamon, Nora, and Nellie. My heart flips for you! —S.W.F.

Designed by Nicole Lazarus, Design Superette

Trade paperback ISBN: 978-1-4263-3812-0
Reinforced library binding ISBN: 978-1-4263-3813-7

The author and publisher gratefully acknowledge the expert content review of this book by Annie Heffernon, vice president of the Women's Program, USA Gymnastics, as well as the literacy review of this book by Mariam Jean Dreher, professor of reading education, University of Maryland, College Park.

Publisher's Note
Gymnastics skills require plenty of practice! Do not try any of these moves without proper training and adult supervision.

Photo Credits
AS=Adobe Stock; GI=Getty Images
Cover, ssj414/GI; cover (background), dynamic/Shutterstock; top border (throughout), hypergon/GI; vocabulary art (throughout), lamnee/AS; 1, Iain Scott Photography/Alamy Stock Photo; 3, Michael Gray/AS; 5, Iain Scott Photography/Alamy Stock Photo; 6, G. Dagli Orti/DeAgostini/GI; 6-7, Vladimir Wrangel/Shutterstock; 8-9, Bettmann/GI; 9, ullstein bild/ullstein bild via GI; 11, nycshooter/GI; 13 (UP), _italo_/AS; 13 (LO), JackF/AS; 14 (UP LE), Mike Kemp/Alamy Stock Photo; 14 (UP RT), Alex Bogatyrev/Shutterstock; 14 (LO), Jiang Dao Hua/Shutterstock; 17 (UP), Francois Nel/GI for BEGOC; 17 (LO LE), Dominique Douieb/GI; 17 (LO RT), master1305/AS; 18 (UP), Alex Koch/AS; 18 (CTR), Paul Vathis/AP/Shutterstock; 18 (LO), Simon Bruty/Sports Illustrated via GI/GI; 19 (UP), bmcent1/GI; 19 (CTR LE), HAYKIRDI/GI; 19 (CTR RT), Ashmolean Museum/Heritage Images/GI; 19 (LO), Yolandagarciafoto/AS; 20, oleg66/GI; 21 (LE), SDI Productions/GI; 21 (RT), Robert Kneschke/AS; 22, Ezra Shaw/GI; 23, Patrick Smith/GI; 24, Thomas Barwick/GI; 25, CasarsaGuru/GI; 26, Alistair Berg/GI; 27 (UP), RichLegg/GI; 27 (LO), CasarsaGuru/GI; 28-29, Dan Mullan/GI; 30 (UP), Thomas Barwick/GI; 30 (CTR), bauhaus1000/GI; 30 (LO, diving board), wellphoto/AS; 30 (LO, pencil), rvlsoft/Shutterstock; 30 (LO, brick), Shawn Hempel/Shutterstock; 30 (LO, notebook), Mark Thiessen/NGP staff; 31 (UP LE), katatonia82/Shutterstock; 31 (UP RT), Greg Trott/GI; 31 (LO LE, bars), huaxiadragon/AS; 31 (LO LE, pommel), caluian/AS; 31 (LO LE, rings), mehmetcan/AS; 31 (LO LE, beam), polhansen/AS; 31 (LO RT), mehmetcan/AS; 32 (UP LE), polhansen/AS; 32 (UP RT), Robert Decelis Ltd/GI; 32 (CTR LE), Allison Zaucha for the Washington Post via GI; 32 (CTR RT), Dan Mullan/GI; 32 (LO LE), Bettmann/GI; 32 (LO RT), Alex Bogatyrev/Shutterstock

National Geographic supports K–12 educators with ELA Common Core Resources. Visit natgeoed.org/commoncore for more information.

Printed in the United States of America
20/WOR/1

Table of Contents

Flipping Out!	4
Jump Back in Time	6
All-Around Fun!	10
7 Cool Facts About Gymnastics	18
In Training	20
Get in Gear	26
In It to Win It	28
Quiz Whiz	30
Glossary	32

Flipping Out!

In a gym, a boy runs across a bouncy floor. He flips in the air and lands on two feet.

Nearby, a girl is on a beam. She kicks into a handstand. As she balances, she does a split.

Running, flipping, and balancing: Gymnasts use these skills to perform in different events. Sometimes it seems like they can fly!

Tumble Talk

EVENT: A gymnastics contest that takes place on a certain piece of equipment

Jump Back in Time

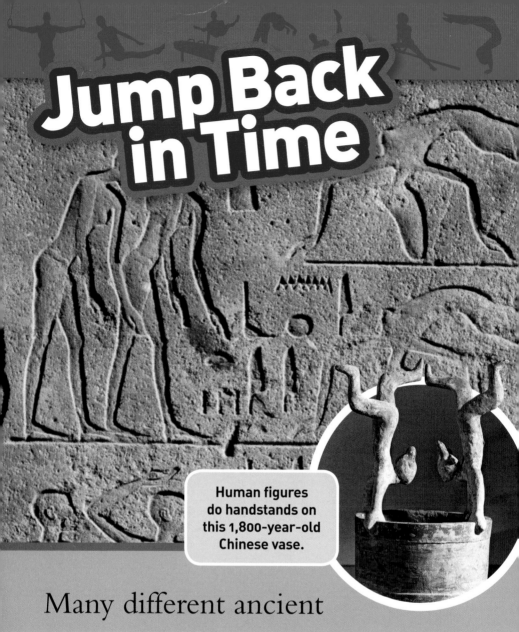

Human figures do handstands on this 1,800-year-old Chinese vase.

Many different ancient (AYN-shunt) cultures practiced gymnastics. Artwork from thousands of years ago in Egypt and China shows people doing tumbling moves.

This stone carving is from an ancient temple in Luxor, Egypt.

In ancient Greece, soldiers (SOLE-jurz) used gymnastic moves to get ready for war. They would practice jumping on and off their horses.

7

People in ancient Greece also competed in the first Olympic Games. The ancient games included gymnastics events! Back then, only men were allowed to compete.

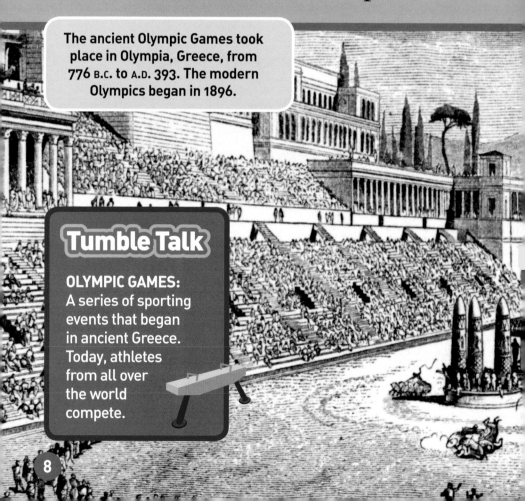

The ancient Olympic Games took place in Olympia, Greece, from 776 B.C. to A.D. 393. The modern Olympics began in 1896.

Tumble Talk

OLYMPIC GAMES: A series of sporting events that began in ancient Greece. Today, athletes from all over the world compete.

Almost 3,000 years later, women's gymnastics was added to the modern Olympic Games.

Women first competed in gymnastics at the Olympic Games in 1928. This photo shows a German gymnast who competed at the 1936 Olympics.

All-Around Fun!

Gymnasts perform in different events. Each event is done on a special apparatus (AP-uh-RAT-us). Gymnastics routines (roo-TEENZ) are up to 90 seconds long. They end with a skill called a dismount— even if you're on the floor and not getting off any apparatus!

Tumble Talk

APPARATUS:
A piece of equipment used in gymnastics, such as the balance beam or the floor

ROUTINE:
A series of gymnastic moves that show a range of skills on one apparatus

DISMOUNT:
A skill used to end a routine or to get off an apparatus after a routine

In gymnastics, there are eight kinds of events.

Floor: A gymnast performs flips, handstands, cartwheels, and somersaults (SUM-ur-salts) on a square mat.

Parallel Bars: A gymnast grips two bars that are parallel (PARE-uh-lel), or an even amount of space away from each other. The routine includes handstands, holds, and one-armed twists.

floor

parallel bars

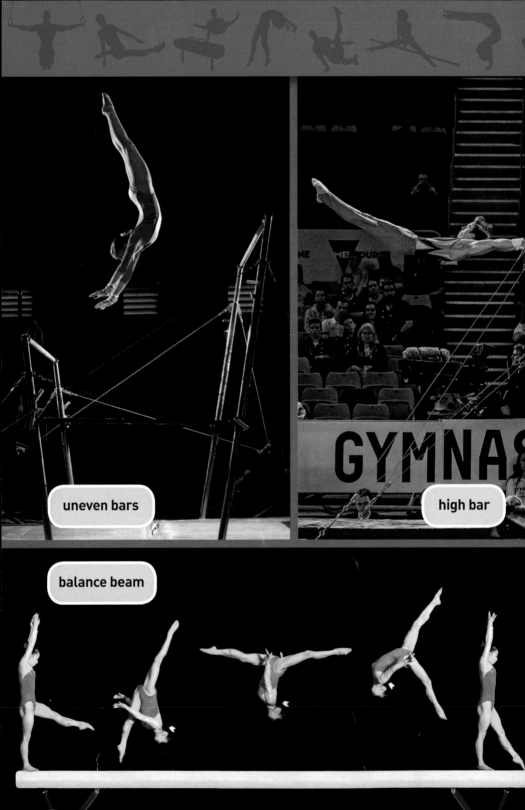

uneven bars

high bar

GYMNA

balance beam

Uneven Bars: A gymnast performs on a pair of bars that are set at different heights. The gymnast moves between the bars, doing handstands and spins.

High Bar: A gymnast grips a bar that is set high off the ground. The gymnast swings around the bar to gain speed, then does twists and flips.

Balance Beam: A gymnast balances on a narrow beam while performing leaps, turns, and flips.

15

Vault: A gymnast runs and bounces off a springboard onto a wide platform, then flips or twists in the air before landing.

Pommel Horse: A gymnast grips two handles, or pommels (POM-ulz), that are on top of a narrow platform called a horse. The gymnast performs skills while swinging above the horse.

Rings: A gymnast grips a set of hanging rings and performs a series of swings and strength holds.

vault

pommel horse

rings

7 COOL FACTS
About Gymnastics

1 A man once completed 67 cartwheels in one minute—a world record.

2 In 1976, Nadia Comaneci (kom-uh-NECH) of Romania scored the first ever perfect 10 at the Olympics.

3 U.S. gymnast Simone Biles was the first woman to land a triple-twisting double backflip in a floor routine during competition. The move is now named the Biles II.

National Gymnastics Day is celebrated every September in the United States.

4

A balance beam is four inches wide, about as wide as a brick.

5

In ancient Greece, athletes would flip over the back of a bull for sport. This move was similar to how gymnasts use a vault today.

6

In gymnastics, a back handspring is also called a flic-flac.

7

In Training

It takes plenty of practice to master a gymnastics skill. Gymnasts spend a lot of time working on each event. They also spend a lot of time working out.

Gymnasts have to be strong. Exercises like pull-ups, push-ups, and sit-ups help build muscles.

Gymnasts have to be flexible, too. They become more flexible by stretching every single day.

Gymnasts also work hard on their dismounts. It's important to "stick" the landing. This means landing on two feet without taking a step in any direction, as if your feet are stuck to the floor with glue. It takes good balance to stick the landing.

Safety comes first in the gym. Before practicing, gymnasts always warm up. They run around and stretch. This gets their muscles loose and ready to perform their routines. Warming up helps prevent injuries.

Q How long does it take a gymnast to get to practice?

A A split second!

In the gym, each apparatus is surrounded by mats and foam pits. These create soft landing spots so gymnasts don't get hurt if they fall.

25

Get in Gear

Gymnasts wear close-fitting outfits made of a material called spandex. Spandex is comfortable and stretchy, so it's easy to move around in it.

Gymnasts also use other gear. They use hand grips to protect their skin from blisters. They also cover their hands and grips in chalky powder to get a better hold on the apparatus.

27

In It to Win It

Tumble Talk

FORM: A gymnast's body position

Each event at a gymnastics meet is scored by judges. When scoring, the judges look at the gymnast's form and how hard the routine is.

Judges like to see straight legs and pointed toes. They also want to see the gymnast stick the landing.

You may be in it to win it, or you might just love bouncing around. Either way, gymnastics is something to flip for!

QUIZ WHIZ

How much do you know about gymnastics? After reading this book, probably a lot! Take this quiz and find out.
Answers are at the bottom of page 31.

1

Why is it important for gymnasts to warm up before training?

A. to loosen up their muscles
B. to get ready to perform their routines
C. to prevent injuries
D. all of the above

2

How did some ancient Greeks use gymnastics to get ready for war?

A. They practiced jumping on and off their horses.
B. They did cartwheels across the battlefield.
C. They flipped off of tall walls.
D. They swung around tree branches.

A balance beam is about as wide as _____.

A. a diving board
B. a pencil
C. a brick
D. a notebook

3

4

What do judges look at when scoring an event?

A. the gymnast's form
B. how hard the routine is
C. the landing
D. all of the above

5

What does it mean to "stick" a landing?

A. landing on two feet
B. stumbling after landing
C. putting glue on your feet before landing
D. landing upside down

6

What is a pommel?

A. a skill done on the uneven bars
B. a handle on top of a gymnastics horse
C. a set of hanging rings
D. another word for the balance beam

7

Why do gymnasts cover their hands in chalky powder?

A. for better balance
B. for speed
C. for a better hold on the apparatus
D. for good luck

APPARATUS: A piece of equipment used in gymnastics, such as the balance beam or the floor

DISMOUNT: A skill used to end a routine or to get off an apparatus after a routine

EVENT: A gymnastics contest that takes place on a certain piece of equipment

FORM: A gymnast's body position

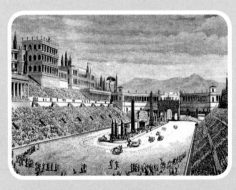

OLYMPIC GAMES: A series of sporting events that began in ancient Greece

ROUTINE: A series of gymnastic moves that show a range of skills on one apparatus